CODEX
TAAWA

+ + + + +

EXPLORING THE
COSMOS OF THE **HOPI**

GERALD DAWAVENDEWA

RIO NUEVO
PUBLISHERS

Rio Nuevo Publishers®
P. O. Box 5250
Tucson, AZ 85703-0250
(520) 623-9558, www.rionuevo.com

Library of Congress Cataloging-in-Publication Data

Names: Dawavendewa, Gerald, artist, author.
Title: Codex Taawa : exploring the cosmos of the Hopi / Gerald Dawavendewa.

Other titles: Exploring the cosmos of the Hopi
Description: Tucson, AZ : Rio Nuevo Publishers, [2021] | Includes
bibliographical references. | Summary: "Dawavendewa's series Codex Taawa
is inspired by ancient imagery that explores the cosmos of the Hopi"—
Provided by publisher.
Identifiers: LCCN 2020056620 | ISBN 9781940322452 (hardback)
Subjects: LCSH: Hopi Indians—Religion. | Hopi art. | Hopi mythology. |
LCGFT: Illustrated works.
Classification: LCC E99.H7 D3775 2021 | DDC 299.7/8458—dc23
LC record available at https://lccn.loc.gov/2020056620

Managing Editor: Aaron Downey
Book design: Katie Jennings Design

Printed in Korea

10 9 8 7 6 5 4 3 2 1

+ + + + +

ARTIST'S STATEMENT

THIS ART SERIES REFLECTS MY OBSERVATIONS AND INTERPRETATIONS of the universe. Each piece highlights a part of the Hopi tradition, stories, or knowledge. The original artworks are black and copper ink on handmade Nepalese Lhakpa Paper.

This series is inspired by the Codices of Mesoamericans. These screen-fold, or accordion-fold, manuscripts are often elaborately illustrated with character or symbol writing. Only twelve of what may have been thousands are known to have survived.

I grew up in the Hopi village of Munqapi, located in the desert of Northern Arizona, and with Cherokee relatives in the deep woods of Oklahoma. I remember the night skies. With little outdoor lighting at Munqapi and none at my Cherokee grandparents' home, the night sky was overwhelming, with every space filled with stars, planets, meteors, the Milky Way, and the Moon.

For the Hopi, the night sky is an astronomical calendar with all of its elements used to set ceremonies, rituals, seasons, events, and measures of time. The Hopi people have observed and measured the movements in the sky to create a complex guide to assist them with existing in this world, which we know as Tuuwaqatsi—the Fourth World.

CODEX
TAAWA

8

MUUYAW MÓMOKI

The Moon Becoming Eclipsed

Taawa crosses the sky. There is a time when
Muuyaw travels opposite of Taawa, bringing
them face-to-face, and Tuuwaqatsi stands
between them. Taawa brings light to the Fourth
World that does not shine full upon Muuyaw.

10

MUUYAWKATSINA

Lunar Spirit

Moon Katsina is a spirit from outer space and is an important figure within Hopi religion. The spirit guards people at night and announces the time for Hopi ceremonies. Muuyawkatsina also assists in maintaining balance in the universe.

12

WORLDS

This art represents the creation of the world by Taawa, who found the first world imperfect and therefore destroyed it into a blackened world.

A second world was created, but it too was seen as imperfect, so it was destroyed by water covering the world.

A third world was then created. Taawa chose to let that world exist even as the people on the planet became corrupt and prideful. The few who still followed the path of Taawa began searching for a way to leave the corrupt world. Through the help of plants and animals and prayers, they traveled upon a reed and ascended into this world, Tuuwaqatsi, the Fourth World.

SIPÀAPUNI

Sipàapuni is the emergence point to Tuuwaqatsi.
A migration spiral enters Tuuwaqatsi, which holds
a ladder representing the passage to the Fourth
World. Stars gather in the darkness, the "roof" of the
Third World. The circle with inner circles depicts a
spiritual being—the guardian of Tuuwaqatsi. A staff
with dots represents the three previous worlds.

PASSAGE

A migration pathway forms a doorway to a star-filled sky, a passage from one world to another.

18

+ 06 +

THE CENTER OF TUUWAQATSI

The cross is the spiritual center with the inner
place—the Earth's center. It is the place the Hopi
came to after great migrations to the four directions
as they traveled to the edge of the land, to the
edge of the sand, and to the edge of the water.
Above the Taawa, Muuyaw and the planets guided
the clans to the center, blessed by rain clouds.

19

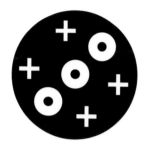

+ 07 +

PÀAYO' MAANAT

Three Maidens, Stars in the Sky

The constellation is named Hotòmqam, the "string up" stars. Other people call them the Belt of Orion in the Orion constellation.

+ 08 & 09 +

PAATUWVATA

Flying Shield

Ancient stories tell of events in which spiritual beings assist Hopi in traveling great distances with the use of devices called Paatuwvata, or Flying Shields. Other stories describe the flying object as gourd-like with the ability to divide in half to allow the passengers to enter and exit.

22

23

24

CLOUD HOUSES

Tuuwaqatsi is surrounded by four cloud houses,
which bring life-giving rains to the world.

+ 11 +

SOLAR ECLIPSE

Muuyaw eclipsed Taawa, darkening Muuyaw. Hisatsinom observed bright swirling lights spreading outward from Taawa, who had hidden behind Muuyaw.

At Yupköyvi, a rock carving depicts a solar corona during a total solar eclipse on July 11, 1097. The Sun created large coronal mass ejections around the dark Moon.

28

MUUYAW PHASES

With Taawa bringing blessings of life-giving
sunlight, Muuyaw migrates around Tuuwaqatsi.
Stars representing the six directions symbolize
the movement of all things in the cosmos.

30

BECOMING A
NEW MOON

Stars watch as Muuyaw is shined upon
by Taawa, revealing a New Moon.

32

POWAMUY

Spiritual being Ahölwutaqa rises with the morning Sun to carry prayers for peace and a long, healthy life. Above, a planet marks the winter solstice with Aaya symbolizing Tuuwaqatsi, the Fourth World. Aaya is decorated with prayer feathers fanning outward to the four directions. The rattle, when shaken, resonates with inner sounds of the Earth.

33

34

+ **15** +

SUPER NOVA

A great light appeared near Muuyaw. Its brightness was seen even when Taawa traveled across the sky.

On July 5, 1054, a bright light erupted southeast of the crescent Moon. The Moon was on the eastern horizon of the sunrise that morning. This light was of such brightness that it was seen during the day.

SUPER NOVA IMAGES

The top circle is an ancient village no
longer lived in or planted.

The center circle from stone is located at Hopqöyvi.

The bottom circle Tutuveni is from
Tuuwanasave, the place where the Hopi clans
have gathered, the center of the Earth.

SOOMALATSI

Star Fingers

Stars shine on Tuuwaqatsi, the Fourth World that we live upon. The hand outstretched to the stars is covered with rain clouds and lightning, signifying life.

This constellation is bright in the western sky during winter. The stars spread outward in all directions like pointing fingers. Others named it Auriga.

39

+ 18 & 19 +

SACRED STAR

There was a great crater from a falling star, and even Hoopoq'yaqam did not know how it came to be. They found parts of a star, which were different from all other stones. The sacred stars were taken to a rock-lined cist and placed into the Earth wrapped in a turkey-feather blanket.

40

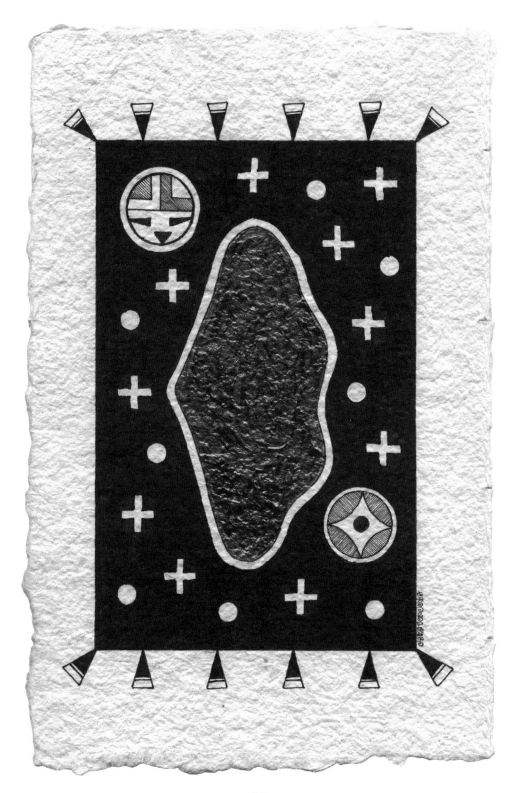

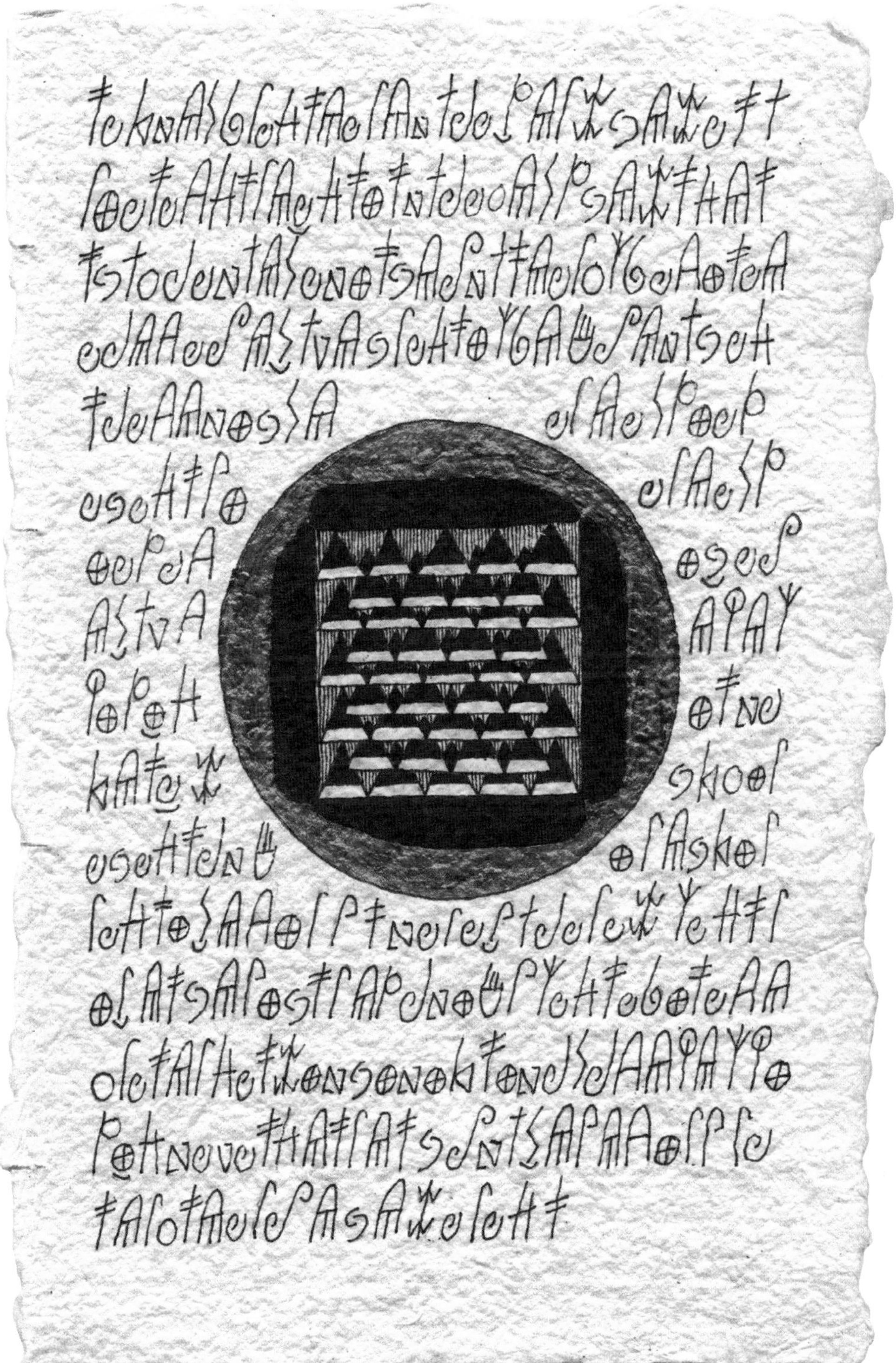

+ 19 +

42

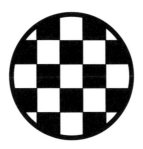

QWAQALALNI

Qwaqalalni marks Tuuwanasave, the center of
the Earth for the Hopi. Boundary stone markers
are a physical reminder of one's commitment
to Taawa and the teachings of Màasaw.

43

44

KIVA

At Hopqöyvi there is a great Kiva that represents Tuuwaqatsi, the Fourth World in which we live. The Kiva marks the clans and the four directions. The Kiva marks the solstice that occurs throughout the year. The Kiva symbolizes the world and the perfect corn ear.

46

+ **22** +

POKSÕ

Taawa journeys across the horizon above
Tuuwaqatsi. Upon Tuuwaqatsi, a tower is built
with an opening at the corner, to observe
the movements of Taawa and Muuyaw.

47

48

TUMALE

Tumale is the work achieved by one's own hands;
it is the work of one person's contribution to
society. The hand holds prayer feathers, clouds, and
lightning, indicating a life of work and prayer.

The hand reaches for the corn, symbolizing a promise
of a challenging but fulfilling life. The Sun radiates
from the sky, acknowledging that the people of the
blue corn have chosen to follow the path of Hopi.

49

NANGOYSÖHUT

Planet Katsina

Chasing and Pursuing Katsinam

Tuuwaqatsi exists surrounded by Tokpela, sky without end. Nangoysöhut spirits traveled together across this endless space. They are the morning and evening star, the planet in the morning light and in the darkness of night. They always travel in pairs, one appearing with Taawa and another with Muuyaw.

For the Hopituh Sinom, Nangoysöhut, also known as Venus, was seen as two separate entities, who are the same katsina spirits.

52

MIGRATION

Wupat'pela holds a migration symbol with four points representing the journey of the ancient people.

+ 28 & 29 +

AAYA

Rattle

Aaya, the rattle, represents the movement of Tuuwaqatsi, the world that we live upon. The center holds the migration of the people and rotation of Tuuwaqatsi. A horizon line of rain clouds bring life-giving moisture. Rays of light from Taawa bring warmth that envelops Tuuwaqatsi. Surrounding the Fourth World is Soongwupa circling through Tokpela. Upon Tuuwaqatsi stand the Warrior Twins at opposite points as they rotate the Fourth World. This is a reminder that we, as people of Tuuwaqatsi, are part of a greater creation.

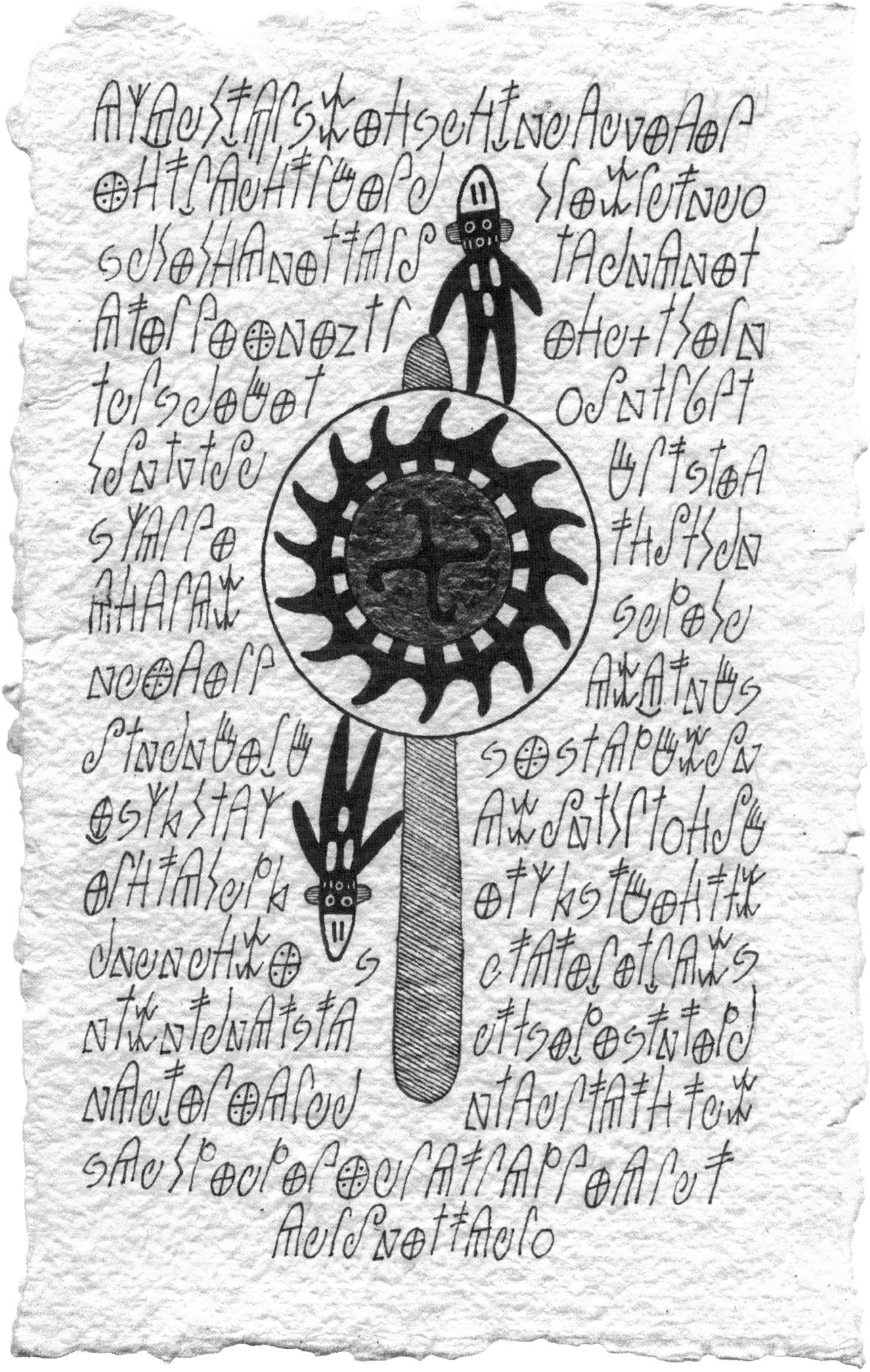

+ 29 +

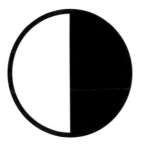

PASSAGE FROM THE FIFTH AND FOURTH WORLD

A perfect blue corn plant grows on a horizon line, separating prayer feathers from dragonflies and butterflies gathered in the Fourth World, announcing the coming rain clouds.

60

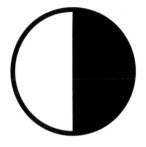

HOOHÒOMANA

Hoohòomana represents the elements of Soonwuqa, the Milky Way. Her voice echoes her name as she journeys throughout the universe.

62

+ **32** +

AHÖLA

An ancient spirit among the Katsinam, Ahöla appears
the morning of the winter solstice, performing a
ceremony with Taawa to bring longer days of sunlight.
Ahöla ends the ceremony with prayers to Taawa to
bring long life, happiness, and blessings for all life.

63

64

QATSI

Six ears of corn mark the six directions, which include
the zenith and the nadir. Corn ears and rain clouds
align with the cardinal directions. The center is
Tuuwaqatsi, the Fourth World, on which we live.

66

TAAWA

Taawa, the Sun, is the creative
force for all living things.

TAAWAKATSINA

Sun Spirit

Taawakatsina represents the spirit of the Sun.

70

+ 36 +

TAAWAVENTIWA

A halo surrounds Taawa as it travels across
the night sky. Above, a planet rises. Below
the Sun, Tuuwaqatsi and Muuyaw follow.

71

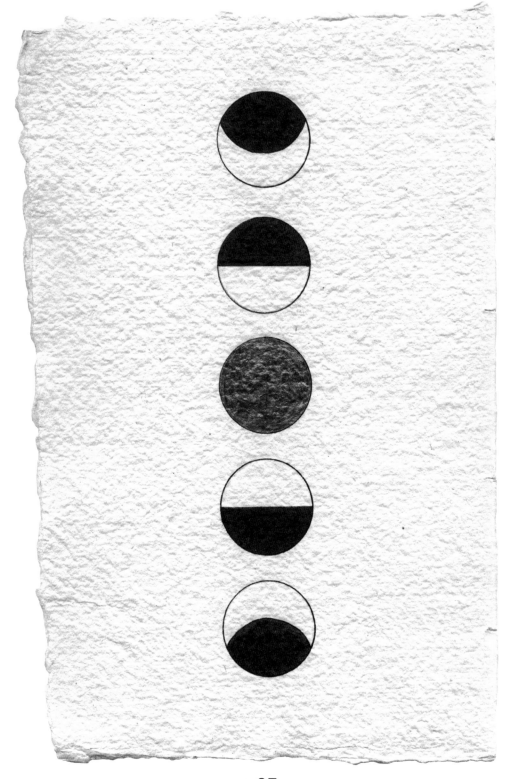

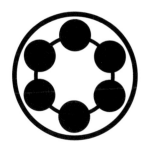

MUUYAW PASSAGES

Muuyaw represents directions in space. It is a
calendar marker and announces the ceremonies.

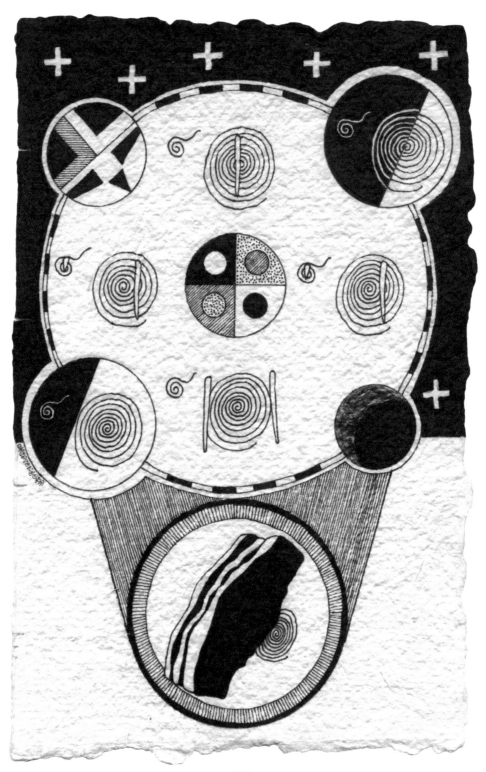

74

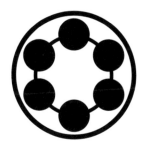

+ 38 +

TAAWATUTUVENI

Sun Calendar

Near Hopqöyvi at Tsa'aktuyqa is a small butte with three stone slabs above a spiral representing the passage of Muuyaw.

Tuuwaqatsi sits at the center, as north shows spiral with light of Taawa shining through stone slabs, marking the summer solstice. To the east is spring equinox, to the south is the winter solstice, and to the west is the fall equinox.

+ 39 & 40 +

SOLSTICE MARKERS

Tutuveni found in caves located in what is now known as the Petrified Forest area.

76

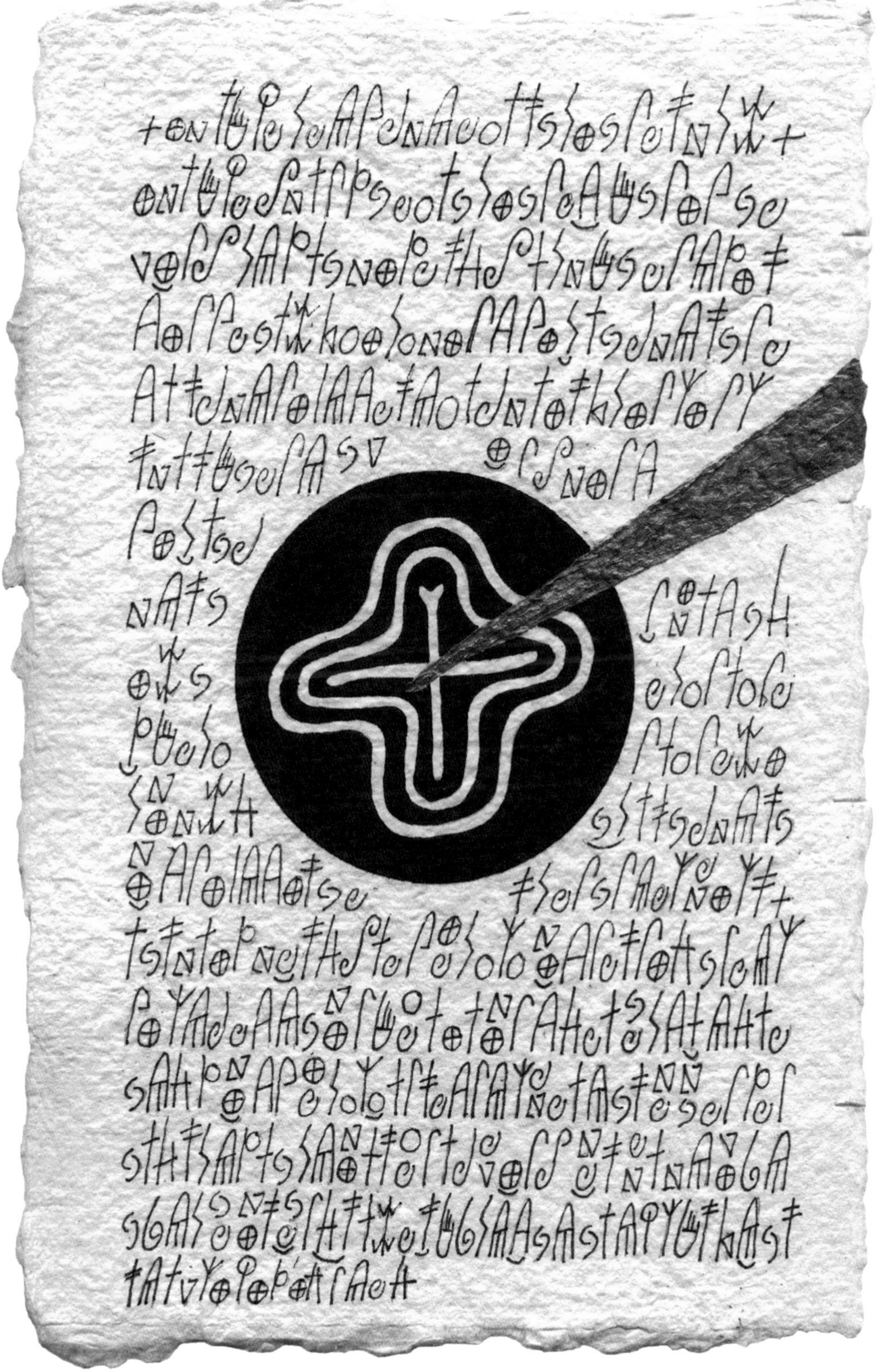

+ 40 +

TALWÌIPIKI

Lightning filament strikes a sacred corn ear, giving life to the land. Crossing from a star-filled night sky to the morning, butterflies gather, symbolized as flowers announcing the coming rain.

MIGRATION PRAYERS

A prayer feather for good blessings and journeys travels with a migration symbol to Tuuwaqatsi between the day and night. It is a prayer for all upon Tuuwaqatsi.

MIGRATION OF CLANS

When Hopi people emerged into Tuuwaqatsi,
they began migration journeys into the four
directions, creating clans as they traveled.

SOOTUKWNANGW

Sootukwnangw is a spiritual Star Being
who brings balance to the universe.

He arrives in the village, and each step is carefully
placed upon the ground; each step is deliberate. He
slowly ascends to the top of the Kiva. His prayer is quiet;
its song flows through the morning air. With an upward
thrust, lightning arches into the air, then with his other
hand he holds out a Tovokìnpi. Unclasped, it unwinds to
the ground stopping moments before the sandstone.
Thunder fills the air, announcing the lightning. He
straightens his arm outward, and the Tovokìnpi spins and
wraps around his hand until it arrives into his palm and
he closes his hand. He turns and descends the Kiva and
moves to the next. Each move, each gesture, is perfect.

PÀAYO'

Two stars gather near Muuyaw. They are the
brightest in the night sky. Muuyaw brings blessings,
symbolized by moisture and prayer feathers.

88

MORNING STAR

Shining upon Taawaqatsi, it is the brightest,
as Taawa rises before sunrise.

MIGRATION OF CLANS, MIGRATION OF ONE

This represents the journey of the clans and of a person's own journey through this world. In the center of the black lines is the emergence point, when the people first arrived into Tuuwaqatsi, the Fourth World. The clans journeyed outward to the four directions, exploring the world, but eventually returned to Tuuwanasave, the center of the universe for the Hopi. The inner white line is the journey of the person. Each turn represents significant moments in life. When you have reached outward and leave the design, you have passed from this world to the next. Above the opening, a line rises upward symbolizing the four major ages in life: child, youth, adult, and elder.

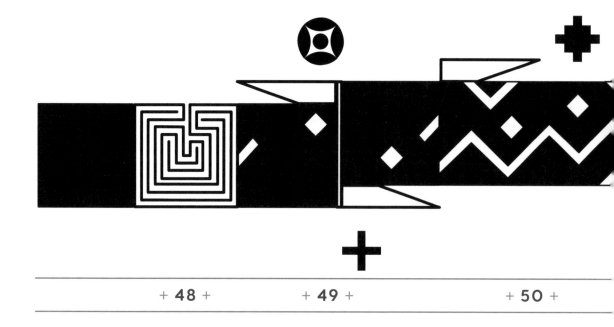

+ 48 +

MIGRATION WORLDS

Two worlds, Taawa destroyed. The Third World
became corrupted. Those who followed Taawa
left to the Fourth World, migrating into the four
directions until reaching the center of the universe.

+ 49 +

SOONGWUPA

Celestial elements cross Soongwupa, who holds
prayer feathers, promises of life with blessings.

+ 50 +

STAR HOUSE

Sohu travels with Soongwupa

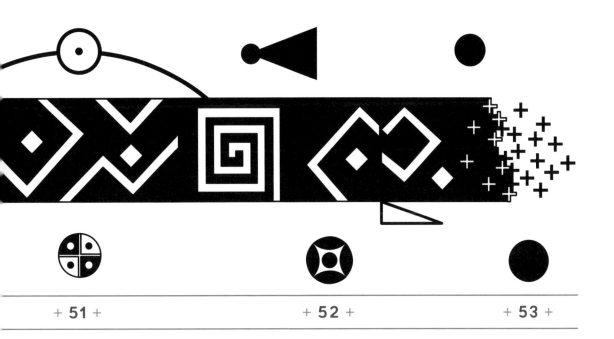

+ 51 +

MUUYAW AND TUUWAQATSI

Muuyaw and Tuuwaqatsi travel throughout Tokpela. Crossing their path is Soongwupa with corn seeds, the promise of life.

+ 52 +

SHOOTING STAR

A shooting star crosses Soongwupa and another star. Soongwupa holds the promise of germination and a symbol of migration to represent the journeys of the cosmos through Tokpela.

+ 53 +

TRAIL OF SOONGWUPA

Among ancient suns, stars create the Milky Way.

94

96

+ + + + +

BIBLIOGRAPHY

Hopi Dictionary Project. 1998. Hopi Dictionary. Tucson: University of Arizona Press.

Malville, J. McKim, and Claudia Putnam. 1989. *Prehistoric Astronomy In the Southwest*. Boulder: Johnson Publishing Company.

Moore, Patrick. 1985. *Stargazing: Astronomy Without a Telescope*. Cambridge: Cambridge University Press.

Museum of Northern Arizona. 2006. *Plateau, the Land & People of the Colorado Plateau: Murals & Metaphors*. Fall 2006, Volume 3, Number 1. Flagstaff: Museum of Northern Arizona.

Secakuku, Alph H. 1995. *Following the Sun and Moon: Hopi Kachina Tradition*. Phoenix: The Heard Museum.

Williamson, Ray A. 1984. *Living the Sky: The Cosmos of the American Indian*. Norman: University of Oklahoma Press.

GLOSSARY

Aaya: *Rattle*

Ahöla: *Spiritual being who appears during the winter solstice.*

Hisatsinom: *Ancient people that the Hopi people came from Hotòmqam. Orion.*

Hopituh Sinom: *Hopi.*

Hopoq'yaqam: *Ancient people.*

Hopqöyvi: *Ancient place that is said to be Chaco Canyon.*

Katsina: *Spiritual being.*

Kiva: *Structure built for ceremonies and community functions.*

Màasaw: *Spiritual being who is the guardian of the Fourth World, life, and death.*

Muuyaw: *Earth's moon.*

Muuyawkatsina: *Lunar spiritual being.*

Nangoysöhut: *Spiritual being referencing Venus.*

Poksõ: *Window, ventilating hole.*

Qatsi: *Life, existence.*

Sipàapuni: *Opening to this world, the Earth.*

Soomalatsi: *Auriga constellation.*

Soongwupa: *The Milky Way.*

Sootukwnangw: *Spiritual star being who brings balance to the universe.*

Taawa: *Sun, the creative force for all living things.*

Taawatutuveni: *Center of the Earth.*

Taawaventiwa: *Rainbow or halo around the Sun.*

Talwìipiki: *Lightning filament.*

Tokpela: *Sky.*

Tovokìnpi: *Bullroarer.*

Tutuveni: *Visual or written symbols.*

Tuuwaqatsi: *Earth, the Fourth World.*

ABOUT THE ARTIST

A member of the Hopi tribe, **GERALD DAWAVENDEWA** grew up in the Hopi village of Munqapi and the Cherokee woods of Oklahoma. His interest in art led to a bachelor's degree in Fine Art from the University of Arizona. Gerald has worked with the Arizona State Museum as an exhibit specialist where he assisted with the development and construction of a 10,000-square-foot exhibit entitled "Paths of Life: American Indians of the Southwest." As part of the exhibit, Gerald painted a mural entitled "Fourth World," which is a permanent part of the museum collection. The logo for the exhibit was later accepted as the official logo for this 124-year-old institution. Gerald interned with the National Museum of American Indian at the Smithsonian Institute. This internship led him to write and illustrate a children's book entitled *The Butterfly Dance*.

In 1994, in partnership with NASA and the University of Arizona, Gerald was honored to be asked to create artwork depicting the Hopi cosmos, which was sent into space aboard the Space Shuttle *Endeavour* (STS-59).

For the University of Arizona's new Student Union complex, Gerald created a series of panels containing native imagery for the main staircase. Other work includes a six-foot-tall sculpture of a parrot that illuminates from within. This project was part of Tucson Pima Arts Council's "Luminarias del Pueblo."

Through his artwork, Gerald hopes to share his cultures, educate the public about the rich heritage of native nations, and promote a greater understanding of the indigenous world.